JOHN JAMES
AUDUBON

PLATE CCCLXVII.

Band-tailed Pigeon, 1. Male. 2. Female.
COLUMBA FASCIATA, Say.
Plant Nuttall Cornel.
Cornus Nuttalli. Aud.

Drawn from Nature by J. J. Audubon, F. R. S. F. L. S.

Engraved, Printed and Coloured by R. Havell. 1837.

JOHN JAMES AUDUBON

MARGOT KEAM CLEARY

JG PRESS

Page 1: Red-bellied Woodpecker/Northern Flicker/Lewis's Woodpecker/Yellow-bellied Sapsucker/Hairy Woodpecker.

Page 2: Band-tailed Pigeon.

Pages 4-5: Spruce Grouse.

NOTE: The latest common English names of the American Birding Association (*ABA Checklist*, 4th ed., 1990) are used for identification in this book.

Published by World Publications Group, Inc.
455 Somerset Avenue
North Dighton, MA 02764
www.wrldpub.com

Copyright © 2004 World Publications Group, Inc.

ISBN 1-57215-360-1

Printed and bound in China by Leefung-Asco Printers Trading Ltd
1 2 3 4 5   06 05 03 02

Contents

PLATE CLXXVI.

Spotted or Canada Grouse.
TETRAO CANADENSIS.
Males 1 Females 2
3 Trillium pictum. 4 Streptopus dictortus

INTRODUCTION

From the time he was just a young boy growing up in France, John James Audubon had a passion for nature. Hours that he should have spent in school were instead passed in the woods and fields near his home, where young Audubon searched out the birds and other creatures he was so fond of. He would collect such treasures as eggs and feathers and nests, and then bring them home and arrange them carefully in his room. These are the pastimes of many youngsters, of course, but Audubon's case was different, for he was blessed with the talent and temperament to transform those childhood interests into works of art. Audubon's lifelong mission, which he accomplished despite the most trying conditions, was "to copy nature, to possess all the production of nature." In his paintings he would render birds faithfully and dramatically. The result was *The Birds of America*, a masterwork of 435 paintings of virtually all known American species, which is still regarded as one of the greatest achievements in American art. With the founding of the National Audubon Society in 1886, thirty-five years after his death, Audubon's unique contribution to nature study would be firmly rooted in the American consciousness.

Mystery surrounds Audubon's earliest years, and he himself fueled the speculation about his lineage. Though his mother's name was never ascertained, he spoke of her as having great wealth as well as beauty. Occasionally he even hinted that he was the lost Dauphin of France, spirited away during the French Revolution and raised by an adoptive family. It is generally accepted, however, that Jean Jacques Audubon (he eventually became known as John James) was born on April 26, 1785, on the island of Santo Domingo (now Haiti) to Jean Audubon, a French sea captain who had holdings in the Americas, and his Creole mistress. Audubon, a younger half-sister, and their father lived on the island until a peasant uprising in 1789 sent them rushing back to the safety of France. Captain Audubon brought his two children to Nantes, and presented them to his wife who cared for them as if they were her own.

But revolt was in the air in France as well as in Santo Domingo, and the Audubon family took haven at *La Gerbetière*, their country home in the south of France. Political necessity turned out to be a personal blessing for young Audubon, who was enchanted by the life he discovered in the nearby woods and fields. He would spend entire days out exploring, and then come home and try to draw what he had seen. His efforts discouraged him but he was a determined and spirited youngster who would never outgrow his fascination with nature, and with birds especially.

The work of philosopher Jean Jacques Rousseau, who exalted nature over civilization, was popular in France at the time, and Audubon's stepmother encouraged his interest in his natural surroundings. The boy spent happy days gathering every nest, egg, bit of moss, and flower blossom he could find, often at the expense of his formal education. The schooling he did receive tended toward the artistic – dancing, music, and fencing – and the young gentleman excelled at them all. But Captain Audubon had a more practical bent. He felt his son should be a seaman like himself, and so when the boy was 14 he sent him to a French military academy. Audubon had already proved himself a lively and free spirit on the many occasions when he skipped school to go scavenging, so the discipline at his new school didn't sit well with him. Much of the year he spent there was devoted to attempts to escape.

Eventually Audubon senior acknowledged that he would never make a sailor of his son and decided to encourage his dual interest in art and nature. Audubon later claimed, although it seems doubtful, that his father had sent him to Paris for several months to study with the great French painter David. Certainly, most of his time at *La Gerbetière* once he returned from military school was devoted to drawing. Still, the young man

Left: A portrait of John James Audubon based upon the painting by his sons Victor and John. The painting was probably done around 1841.

Nº 11.

PLATE 53.

Painted Bunting.

1 & 2. Old Males, 3. M. of 1ˢᵗ Years 4. 2ⁿᵈ Years 5. Female.

FRINGILLA CIRIS.

Plant. Prunus Chicasa.

Drawn from Nature & Published by John J. Audubon, F.R.S.E. F.L.S. M.W.S.

Engraved by R. Havell, Junʳ. Printed & Coloured by R. Havell, Senʳ. London, 1831.

Right: Painted Bunting.

needed to earn a living. In 1803 Audubon set sail for America to manage Mill Grove, a small estate near Philadelphia, Pennsylvania, which his father had purchased some years earlier.

With his fine clothes, handsome appearance, and polished dancing and musicianship, Audubon quickly settled into the social life of the Pennsylvania countryside. And Mill Grove offered abundant opportunities for him to indulge in his hobby: there was a river nearby, and limestone caves, and plenty of woods and fields in which to roam. "Hunting, fishing and draw-

ing occupied my every moment . . . " Audubon later wrote of that happy time, "cares I knew not, and cared nothing for them."

Many of the birds Audubon hunted would end up back in his rooms at Mill Grove, where he would attempt to preserve them in his drawings. But he soon discovered that a dead bird lacked the vibrancy that he so admired in the wild. How could he reproduce that vitality through his art? To the dismay of his domestic help, for whom dead animals were becoming a house-

Left: Mill Grove, his father's farm outside of Philadelphia, Pennsylvania, was Audubon's first home in America.

Below: Audubon's rendition of a whippoorwill from 1806 as compared to his work in *The Birds of America* shows the vast improvement and refinement he made with years of practice.

keeping problem, he spent hours trying to come up with a method that would work. Finally he succeeded. By passing wires through a freshly killed bird, Audubon could pose it so it seemed almost alive again. It was a technique he would rely on for decades to come.

Life at Mill Grove was even more enjoyable once Audubon made the acquaintance of a neighbor, a young Englishwoman named Lucy Bakewell. Audubon, like many Frenchmen of his era, had considerable disdain for everything English, and the fact that he so quickly and wholeheartedly fell in love with Lucy was a testament to her charms. He was determined to marry her.

First, however, there were obstacles to overcome. Perhaps concerned that his son was too much the social butterfly and not enough of a businessman, Audubon senior had sent over a man named Francis Dacosta to help run Mill Grove. It was not a match made in heaven. Audubon was convinced that Dacosta was out to bilk the family, so in 1805 he headed to France to inform his father. The trip had a dual purpose, however. Audubon also hoped to persuade his father to allow him to marry Lucy Bakewell.

He spent much of his year in France working on bird drawings. Dr. Charles D'Orbigny, a family friend who would later gain fame as a paleontologist, offered valuable advice on how Audubon could improve his work, and by the time the young man departed for America again he had completed some 200 drawings of the birds of France. In the meantime Audubon's father had found a potential partner for him, Ferdinand Rozier, and the two sailed together in 1806. Captain Audubon hoped that Rozier's steady, businesslike ways would balance Audubon's carefree nature.

Audubon had succeeded in convincing his father to bless his match with Lucy. Now he had to repeat the task back in America with Lucy's father. William Bakewell liked young Audubon, who was not only charming but a man's man as well

(the two had first encountered each other while hunting). But he wanted more from a prospective son-in-law than charm and a knack for drawing birds, and Audubon's attempts to run Mill Grove weren't proving successful. If he wished to marry Lucy, Bakewell told Audubon, he must first show that he could support her. But a job with a New York export firm run by Bakewell's brother only showed that Audubon was no better suited to life as a clerk than as an estate manager, for he spent as much time roaming the city in search of birds as he did sitting at a desk going over figures. It was time to try another venture.

Audubon had always had the soul of an explorer, and he and Rozier decided that the burgeoning western frontier was ripe for a company that would supply settlers and hunters with the goods they needed. He sold his stake in Mill Grove to Dacosta, and in 1807 Audubon and Rozier left for Kentucky to set up shop in Louisville. Apparently William Bakewell was sufficiently reassured by this endeavor, because in April of 1808, Audubon and Lucy were married in Pennsylvania. They left on the rough journey to Kentucky almost immediately.

Back in Louisville, Audubon's partnership with Rozier gave

him ample opportunity to add to his growing collection of bird sketches. While the latter "minded the store," Audubon traveled to buy goods for their shelves, and the journeys turned out to involve as much hunting as buying. To Rozier's growing frustration, more and more of his partner's time was devoted not to business, but to birds.

Until now Audubon had thought of his obsession with drawing birds – for that was what it was clearly becoming – as nothing more than a hobby. But a chance visit in 1810 from one of the premier American ornithologists of the day, Alexander Wilson, planted a new idea in Audubon's mind. Wilson had come to Louisville seeking subscribers for the book he was preparing on American birds. Audubon was hardly in a financial position to subscribe, but a meeting between the two men proved fruitful for at least one of them. For the first time Audubon realized that his skill at drawing birds might be not just enjoyable, but profitable as well. One look at Wilson's work had convinced him that he was far more skilled than the dour Scot, and he began to formulate his own plan to publish. From now on, his drawings would have a purpose.

Competition was growing stiffer in Louisville, however, and Audubon and Rozier decided it was time to pack up and move their business farther into the frontier. Together with Lucy and the Audubon's new son, Victor, born in 1809, they loaded their goods on to a flatboat and traveled 125 miles down the Ohio River to Henderson, Kentucky. Their new home must have been a shock to the ladylike Lucy, for Henderson was a rude outpost filled with trappers and Indians. But she proved remarkably resilient, a trait that would endure throughout her life, and rejoiced with her husband as he discovered countless birds he had never before seen.

The old pattern of business continued; Rozier ran the store while Audubon roamed the woods in search of new specimens. Within six months it was clear that business was no better in Henderson than it had been in Louisville, and the two men headed out into even rougher country while Lucy stayed behind to work as a governess. On one leg of the rigorous journey, cold weather iced over the river, trapping the party for six weeks. Rozier, Audubon noted in one of the journals he had begun to keep, was miserable: "Like a squirrel in winter quarters with his tail about his nose, he slept and dreamed his time away, being seldom seen except at meals." Audubon, on the other hand, was having a grand time, hunting and fishing for food, observing the skills of their Indian guides, and, of course, making countless drawings of the birds along the river.

The trip was the straw that broke the camel's back for Rozier. In 1811 he bought out Audubon's share in the business and opened his own store in a French settlement in upper Louisiana. Audubon walked all the way from Missouri to Henderson, more than 100 miles, to try to earn a living on his own. He had a brief taste of success when some land dealings turned a profit. But the good times were fleeting. Audubon continued to run the store in Henderson, but his passion for birds undermined any success he might have had as a retailer. A partnership with Lucy's brother in a New Orleans import business was scuttled by the tumult of the War of 1812. And an 1817 attempt by the two men to capitalize on Henderson's growth by building a sawmill and gristmill failed as well: the young town had neither the forests nor the farmland to support it. A boat-building venture also foundered, leaving in its wake a growing

Below left: This crayon portrait was done by Audubon in 1819.

Below: Lucy Audubon, from the miniature by F. Cruikshank, 1835.

Above left: Western Tanager/ Scarlet Tanager. **Above:** Rufous-sided Towee.

trail of angry associates who had been drawn in initially by Audubon's appealing personality. Before long Audubon had declared bankruptcy, and he moved his family to Lucy's sister and brother-in-law's house to escape his creditors.

Through it all, Lucy continued to regard her husband's failures with forbearance, for she considered him a man of extraordinary talent. "Her brave and cheerful spirit accepted all," Audubon wrote, "and no reproaches from her beloved lips ever wounded my heart. With her was I not always rich?"

A disaster as a businessman, Audubon finally decided to rely on his artistic talents to support his family. He began hiring himself out to do portraits, and found a measure of success at last: "Misfortune intensified, or at least developed, my abilities." He took a job as a taxidermist at the Western Museum in Cincinnati, and found time to run a small art school as well. In his spare hours he would refine his bird paintings, finally settling on a technique that combined pastels and watercolors to produce a glowing, rich effect.

It was around this time that Audubon, convinced finally that his talents were considerable, made his momentous decision: he would devote himself entirely to publishing the definitive pictorial work on the birds of America. His book would be com-

prehensive, including all American species. And what was more ambitious, his drawings would be life-size, and would depict the birds in their actual habitats. At a time when most works on ornithology were characterized by static renderings of birds in a size easily accommodated by printers, Audubon's plan was revolutionary.

In 1820 he set out for New Orleans on the first leg of a mission that would occupy the next two decades: discovering and painting every bird in America. Accompanying Audubon was one of his pupils from Cincinnati, Joseph Mason, who despite his age – he was just a teenager – had already demonstrated a remarkable talent for painting flowers and foliage. Audubon had hired him to do the backgrounds of his new works.

"Without any money," Audubon wrote in his journal, "my talents are to be my support and my enthusiasm, my guide in my difficulties, the whole of which I am ready to exert . . . "

The journey down the Mississippi by flatboat was through rough territory, and Audubon, once the image of the country squire, now fell easily into the role of frontiersman, assigned to shoot game for the travelers. One of his first forays, he wrote, yielded "thirty partridges – one wood cock – 27 Grey Squirrel – a Barn Owl – a young Turkey Buzzard." When he wasn't hunting, he was drawing. It wasn't unusual for him to spend many hours perfecting his rendering of a single bird – his drawing of the great white heron would take him nearly a month. To earn a few dollars – and in one case new shoes for himself and Mason – Audubon did chalk portraits of people he encountered along the way.

Even so, the two were nearly penniless when they arrived in New Orleans in January of 1821. Audubon immediately set to work drumming up more portrait business, and before long some of his works were fetching as much as $25. The rest of his time was spent on his growing portfolio. Audubon would stalk the city's meat markets early in the day for freshly shot fowl: not just the usual game birds but woodpeckers, bluebirds, and finches too. In the space of weeks he completed 20 paintings.

When the market for his portraits began drying up Audubon secured a position tutoring the daughter of a wealthy bayou family, and not long after that Lucy and the couple's children (there were now two sons) joined him in Louisiana. Lucy brought with her Audubon's earliest paintings, along with some he'd lost on the trip down the Mississippi. His growth as an artist was striking. His renderings of birds were growing increasingly lifelike, and the paintings showed a surer sense of design and color.

When Lucy found work as a governess, Audubon and Mason traveled upriver to Natchez in search of more portrait commissions as well as the occasional tutoring job. Audubon's dream of publishing a body of work on the birds of America seemed distant at this point in his life, but Lucy stood by him. "My wife

determined that my genius should prevail," Audubon later wrote, "and that my final success as an ornithologist should be triumphant."

It was in Natchez that Audubon and Mason parted company amicably. Audubon's regard for his young assistant was abundant, and he had once written to Lucy that Mason "now draws flowers better than any man probably in America." But his affection and admiration had their limits, apparently; while *The Birds of America* would contain nearly 50 backgrounds done by Mason, Audubon saw to it that the young man's name was removed from the plates.

Natchez was also the site of an educational experience for Audubon. Though he was highly skilled in painting with pastels and watercolors, his knowledge of oils was negligible, so he took lessons from a fellow painter who happened to be in Natchez. Though he would never consider himself accomplished in oils, the medium would serve him well in later years when he took to making copies of some of his most popular wildlife paintings to earn money for his great publishing venture.

Audubon was growing increasingly anxious to find a publisher for the book he dreamed of, and after a short spell in Louisiana he decided to set out for Philadelphia in hopes of drumming up financial support. By now his work was so polished that he had little trouble gaining audiences with the city's noted scientists, naturalists, and artists. He took a lesson with the noted painter Thomas Sully, who admired Audubon's work so much that he refused to charge him for his time. An exhibit at a prestigious academy arranged by Napoleon Bonaparte's nephew Charles elicited much praise, but no financial backers. Attempting a book of full-scale birds was simply too expensive a venture for any publisher to take on.

Undermining Audubon's search for backers were the re-

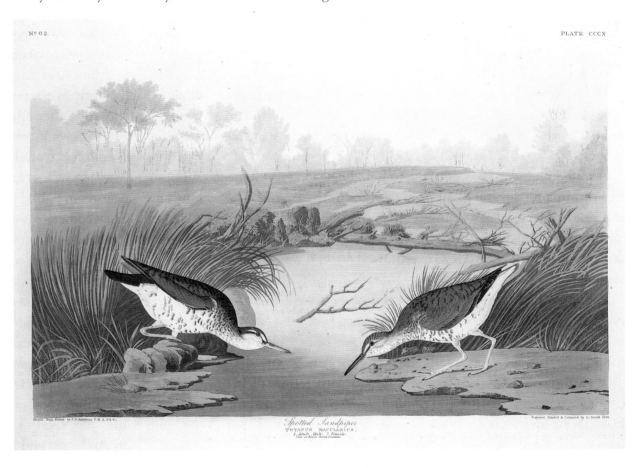

Spotted Sandpiper.

A photograph of Lucy Audubon.

verberations from a single incident years earlier. Perhaps inspired by jealousy, Alexander Wilson had made it clear to his friends in Philadelphia that he cared little for Audubon. Wilson was now dead, but his great work on birds was nearing final publication and his friends wanted nothing to detract from it. They cast a pall over Audubon's work, finding fault with the drama of the poses as well as the highly decorative backgrounds.

Audubon returned to Louisiana to help Lucy at a school she was running for several plantation families in the bayou. The skills he had learned as a youngster in France – music, dancing, and drawing – made him a popular teacher, and since Audubon had plenty of time each day to explore and draw, it was a happy arrangement.

Audubon had returned to Louisiana no better off than he had left it, but with a new resolve. Bonaparte had urged him to take his portfolio to Europe in search of a publisher; only there would it be truly appreciated. Financed by Lucy's now considerable earnings from her school and armed with letters of introduction from scientists and naturalists, Audubon sailed for England in May of 1826. Two months later he arrived in the bustling port of Liverpool.

His introduction to the Rathbones, one of Liverpool's most prominent families, was especially fruitful. Within a week of Audubon's arrival Mr. Rathbone had arranged an exhibit at the Royal Institution of Liverpool, and people crowded to admire bird paintings that were unlike any they had seen before. The English, after all, were accustomed to the work of men like Thomas Bewick, whose woodcuts of birds were accurate yet lacked life. Audubon's image as "the American Woodsman," which he carefully cultivated by wearing his hair long and appearing in public in a fringed buckskin jacket, only added to the newcomer's mystique. Reflecting on his welcome in Liverpool, Audubon wrote, "I am well-received everywhere, my works praised and admired, and my poor heart is at last relieved from the great anxiety that has for so many years agitated it, for I now know that I have not worked in vain."

Edinburgh, too, warmed to the work of the American Woodsman, with one commentator describing his paintings as "a wild and poetical vision of the heart of the new world." And Edinburgh would be where he would finally find a printer. The engraver W.H. Lizars took one look at the American's paintings and said, "My God, I never saw anything like these before!" Soon Audubon and Lizars had entered into an agreement: the engraver would prepare five plates that Audubon would use as samples in his quest for subscribers. The plates would be engraved on copper in double elephant folio format – an expansive 26 by 40 inches – to allow for life-size reproductions of the birds. Lizars would complete 25 plates per year, and the prints pulled from them would then be hand-colored. The full four-volume set was to contain 400 plates (a figure that would ultimately climb to 435). Audubon would finance the work himself by selling subscriptions – 300 of them, he hoped, at roughly $1000 each – and would pay Lizars as each section of the work was completed.

On November 28, 1826, the first of Audubon's plates came off the press. It was the wild turkey, and Audubon was immensely pleased with Lizars's work. By the following February, the remaining four birds in the first group were completed: the yellow-billed cuckoo, the prothonotary warbler, the purple finch, and the Canada warbler. Carrying his new prints, Audubon set out for London in search of subscribers. The success of his great work, he now realized, would depend on his skill at two tasks: creating the paintings for it, and creating demand for it as well.

It was not easy work. While his samples won widespread acclaim (Sir Walter Scott proclaimed them "of the first order"), the steep price put a damper on any number of potential sales. And then, just as the high spirits engendered by his warm receptions in Liverpool and Edinburgh were waning, Audubon received another blow: word from Lizars that the workers who colored the prints had gone on strike. Work on *The Birds of America* had come to a halt.

Audubon was crushed. But the bad news was to prove to be a blessing in disguise. In London he sought out another engraver, and the one he settled on, Robert Havell, Jr., would prove to be eminently suited to the enormous task. Not only was Havell himself interested in zoology, but his work was stunning as well. When Audubon inspected the first plate Havell did for him, of his Baltimore Orioles, he was overjoyed; the birds were close to perfection.

Audubon had signed up only 100 subscribers thus far, and to pay Havell he was forced to fall back on painting oils that he could sell quickly. He would spend his days painting the animal scenes the English seemed to like best – a copy of an otter caught in a trap that he had first done years earlier was among the favorites – and then peddle them in the open-air markets in early evening. Disconsolate, he wrote, "I do anything for money nowadays."

By 1828 Audubon felt he had exhausted the potential English market for his book and headed for France. He met with the great painter of flowers, Pierre Redouté, who praised the animated nature of Audubon's birds and recommended him to the Duc d'Orléans (later to become King Louis-Philippe) who was so impressed with Audubon's Baltimore Oriole plate that he promptly took out subscriptions for both himself and his wife. But despite the admiration Audubon's works elicited in

Below left: A letter from Audubon to Lucy, Liverpool 1826.

Below: A photograph of Robert Havell, Jr., the engraver of Audubon's *The Birds of America*.

wildlife. The time Audubon spent in the woods and at the shore was profitable, for he finished 42 paintings encompassing nearly 100 birds. But the scope of his work was beginning to overwhelm him, and he decided he once again needed the kind of help Joseph Mason had given him years earlier. Audubon hired an artist to paint backgrounds, and he would do so again several more times before his book was completed.

Audubon's written entreaties to Lucy to return to England with him were accomplishing little. That fall he reached Louisiana and took Lucy by surprise as she taught a piano lesson. "I pronounced her name gently, and she saw me, and the next moment I held her in my arms . . . once more we were together." Soon after, it appears, he prevailed upon Lucy to join him in England.

While his wife prepared to leave the teaching career she had enjoyed for years, Audubon used the time for painting. The bayous had always been good hunting grounds for Audubon, and he spent several happy months seeking out specimens of

Evening Grosbeak
FRINGILLA VESPERTINA. Cooper
Old Male 1

Spotted Grosbeak.
FRINGILLA MACULATA.
Male 2.3 Female. 4

Left: Evening Grosbeak/Black-headed Grosbeak.

Below: The title page of Audubon's *Ornithological Biography*.

France, the country wasn't to prove fertile ground for subscriptions. An Audubon exhibit at one French academy was greeted with this sentiment: "*Quel ouvrage! Quel prix!*" (What work! What a price!). The French appreciated the exquisite artistry of Audubon's book but didn't have the pocketbooks to afford it.

By now convinced that he had found all the subscribers he could, Audubon sailed westward in April of 1829. Havell was supplied with enough paintings to keep him busy for some months to come, and Audubon wanted time in America to search out and paint the birds that so far had eluded him and to redraw some of his earlier works. As he wrote to Lucy, "I must draw hard from nature every day that I am in America."

There was another reason he was returning as well. Audubon had missed Lucy immensely and he hoped to persuade her to return to England with him. But she was quite content with her life as a teacher in Louisiana, and he would find that convincing her to give that up would not be easy.

Before he headed for a reunion with Lucy, Audubon had other work to do. For several weeks he camped out in a rough shack in the marshes of New Jersey, on the lookout for such water birds as herons, gulls, and terns. Then it was on to Pennsylvania's Great Pine Swamp, a logging tract that was rich with

ORNITHOLOGICAL BIOGRAPHY,

OR AN ACCOUNT OF THE HABITS OF THE

BIRDS OF THE UNITED STATES OF AMERICA;

ACCOMPANIED BY DESCRIPTIONS OF THE OBJECTS REPRESENTED
IN THE WORK ENTITLED

THE BIRDS OF AMERICA,

AND INTERSPERSED WITH DELINEATIONS OF AMERICAN
SCENERY AND MANNERS.

BY JOHN JAMES AUDUBON, F.R.SS. L. & E.

FELLOW OF THE LINNEAN AND ZOOLOGICAL SOCIETIES OF LONDON; MEMBER OF THE LYCEUM
AND LINNEAN SOCIETY OF NEW YORK, OF THE NATURAL HISTORY SOCIETY OF PARIS, THE
WERNERIAN NATURAL HISTORY SOCIETY OF EDINBURGH; HONORARY MEMBER OF THE
SOCIETY OF NATURAL HISTORY OF MANCHESTER, AND OF THE SCOTTISH ACADEMY OF
PAINTING, ARCHITECTURE, AND SCULPTURE, &c.

EDINBURGH:

ADAM BLACK, 55. NORTH BRIDGE, EDINBURGH;
R. HAVELL JUN., ENGRAVER, 77. OXFORD STREET, AND LONGMAN, REES,
BROWN, & GREEN, LONDON; GEORGE SMITH, TITHEBARR STREET,
LIVERPOOL; T. SOWLER, MANCHESTER; MRS ROBINSON, LEEDS;
E. CHARNLEY, NEWCASTLE; POOL & BOOTH, CHESTER; AND BEILBY,
KNOTT, & BEILBY, BIRMINGHAM.

MDCCCXXXI.

White-rumped Sandpiper.

the many migratory birds that arrived there in the winter. But when word came from Havell that the English subscribers were growing restless, with some even cancelling their subscriptions, Audubon and Lucy packed up and sailed for Liverpool on April 1, 1830. Lucy was to manage their business affairs and the duties of everyday life while Audubon devoted himself to his masterwork.

It was around this time that he decided to take on another task as well. He had always taken copious notes, both scientific and anecdotal, on the birds he drew and the places he had been, and he now proposed to write an *Ornithological Biography* of his birds' "life histories" as a companion text to *The Birds of America*. "I know I am not a scholar," Audubon explained, "but meantime I am aware that no man living has studied them as much as I have done, and with the assistance of my old journals and memorandum – books which were written on the spot, I can at least put down plain truths . . . " Audubon hired a Scottish naturalist, William MacGillivray, to serve as his editor, and spurred on by news of a new edition of Alexander Wilson's book the two men dedicated themselves to their task, sometimes working as many as 16 hours each day. Audubon had every confidence that his works on birds would easily be the match of Wilson's. "Wilson has had his day, thought I to myself, and now is my time." His bravura turned out to be justified. Audubon and MacGillivray completed their first volume in just three months (the entire five-volume work would eventually take nine years), and its engaging combination of scientific observation and "Episodes" culled from Audubon's journals was hailed as a masterly achievement.

With Robert Havell and William MacGillivray tending to *The Birds of America* and the *Ornithological Biography*, in 1831 Audubon once again returned to America to seek out both birds and subscribers. In South Carolina (where some years

earlier Mark Catesby had earned acclaim for his elegant bird paintings) he met the Rev. John Bachman, who was a naturalist as well as a minister, and the two began a friendship that would last the rest of Audubon's life. Then Audubon headed for Florida, where he encountered an abundance of new species: pelicans, purple herons, egrets, flamingos, and more. The trip yielded more than just paintings, however, it was also filled with adventures that ended up as more "Episodes," such as Audubon's encounter with unsavory pirates who finally won him over by sharing with him their collections of shells, eggs, and corals. But if Audubon was gaining a look at the colorful side of life, it wasn't without its rigors. He described one day in the Florida Keys like this: "The boat is anchored and we go wading through mud and water amid myriads of sand-flies and mosquitoes, shooting here and there a bird, or squatting down on our hams for half an hour, to observe the ways of the beautiful beings we are in pursuit of."

Audubon was determined that his book would be all-encompassing – it was, after all, titled *The Birds of America* – and not long after leaving Florida he set out for the continent's northern reaches, chartering a schooner out of Maine to take him to Labrador. There he was able to study several gulls that had so far eluded him, along with a number of other water birds, and by the end of the journey he had completed 23 drawings. But by now his age (he was nearly 50) was beginning to catch up with him. The rigors of the trip – it was so cold that Audubon could barely feel his pencil in his hands – received nearly as much space in his journal as the birds he observed.

Audubon would undertake several more expeditions in his quest to capture on paper every known species of bird in America, but he was never able to realize his goal of reaching the Far West. Fortunately, that gap was filled by Thomas Nuttall and John Kirk Townsend, scientists who had traversed

much of the Rockies. The pair sold nearly 100 of the skins of birds they had collected to Audubon at what he considered a most reasonable price, and he was able to paint a number of western birds he had never seen himself.

When he wasn't out hunting for birds, or at John Bachman's home in Charleston working on his paintings, Audubon traveled back and forth to England to provide Havell with more paintings and reassure his subscribers there. While he was away he would implore Bachman to send him birds pickled in rum so he could continue to paint. "I am growing old fast," Audubon observed around this period, "and must work at a double-quick time now."

Audubon's single-minded dedication would soon bear fruit: his two great works would be completed by the end of the 1830s. On June 20, 1838, the last of the 435 plates of *The Birds of America* came off the press. And despite a difficult time with it ("I would rather go without a shirt . . . through the whole of the Florida swamps in mosquito time," he wrote, "than labour as I have hitherto done with the pen"), the *Ornithological Biography* was completed less than a year later. Audubon had captured a continent of birds in pencil and paint, and had done so with a degree of artistry that had never before been seen. In the summer of 1839 he made what would be his last crossing back to America, ". . . my journeys all finished, my anxieties vanished, my mission accomplished."

Even though Audubon had taken in more than $100,000 over the course of his labors, the publication of *The Birds of America* in its unique double elephant folio size would not make him a rich man. He had fallen about 100 subscribers short of his goal of 300, and most of the money he had received from subscribers had gone right back out to pay Havell. But upon his re-

Above: Audubon's house on Riverside Drive in New York City.

Right: A photograph of Audubon by Mathew Brady.

turn to America, Audubon authorized a smaller version of *The Birds of America* to be published in 1843, and at the more affordable price of $100 a copy it sold remarkably well.

The year 1843 was also the date of what would be Audubon's final expedition. In search of animals for a book on viviparous quadrupeds (four-footed animals that give birth to living young) he and Rev. Bachman had long planned, Audubon traveled west to the Yellowstone River, where he saw enough of the condition of the buffalo to warn of its imminent demise. He had used his profits from the miniature version of *The Birds of America* to buy a home – a home capable of holding the entire family, as Lucy had always wanted – in New York City overlooking the Hudson River. Upon his return from this last trip to the west Audubon and Lucy settled down at last. There, in a park-like setting filled with birds and animals, he lived out the rest of his life. With the help of his sons and Bachman he worked on *The Viviparous Quadrupeds of North America* until his eyesight, and then his mind, began to fail. Audubon died at age 65 on January 27, 1851.

He left behind a body of work – not just his exquisitely accurate and exciting paintings, but his wry accounts of both animals and man – that is still regarded as the benchmark for all naturalists who have followed. A visitor who met with Audubon shortly before his death made an observation that remains true even today: "He belongs to all time. He was born, but he can never die."

Mocking Bird. TURDUS POLYGLOTTUS, Linn. Males 1 Females, 2. Florida Jessamine Gelseminum nitidum

PERCHING BIRDS

Audubon's mockingbird painting is one of his most famous. But its fame is derived not just from the way it strikingly illustrated the artist's mastery of composition, color, and action. When the mockingbird plate made its appearance in *The Birds of America* it elicited a storm of controversy that challenged Audubon's integrity.

Fond of the dramatic gesture in his personal life – when he finally cut off his long "American Woodsman" hair while in England, he mourned its loss by drawing a black border around his journal entry for that day – Audubon was just as dramatic in the way he portrayed his birds. He showed them as they lived, not as they looked when stuffed and mounted. To Audubon, it wasn't just the sight of a specimen that appealed to him; it was the sweetness of its song, the places it lived, how it raised its young, where it found its food. His paintings of birds reflect the scope of his interest. His black-billed cuckoos, for example, flutter about a magnolia tree that bears not just fresh blossoms but faded ones as well, and his blue jays feast hungrily on eggs they have stolen from the nest of another bird. It was a radical approach to ornithological art, and one that didn't sit well with some members of the scientific establishment at the time. They were accustomed to images of birds drawn not from life but from faded museum specimens. Endowing birds with movement and drama and presenting them in almost anthropomorphic terms, as Audubon did, marked the beginning of a new way of looking at wildlife.

Audubon's mockingbird plate depicts a family of the birds defending their young from a rattlesnake entwined in the branches of the jessamine (or jasmine) tree where the birds have nested. The painting is one of Audubon's best, illustrating his command of color and design. The striking blacks, grays, and whites of the birds, with just a hint of blue, are set off by the yellow flowers of the jessamine tree. But what makes the scene so unforgettable is the life or death confrontation it presents: the mockingbirds, beaks open and wings spread, are ready to do battle with the sinister reptile. The frightening immediacy of the snake, poised within striking distance of the mockingbird nest, its fangs bared, would bring the debate over Audubon's unconventional bird portraits to a head. He was called a charlatan by scientists on both sides of the Atlantic, particularly by the supporters of the era's other great illustrator of American birds, Alexander Wilson. The painting was fake, Audubon's critics claimed, on several counts. Rattlers, everyone knew, do not climb trees. Nor, they announced, do they have curved fangs. Audubon had obviously concocted the scene in his imagination to lend sensationalism to his work.

Judging from the detailed descriptions of rattlesnakes in Audubon's journals, it is unlikely that he would have fabricated details that were not true to nature. While in the Louisiana bayou country he had studied a rattlesnake specimen most carefully, dissecting the jaw bones to examine the ligaments and counting the precise number of scales from the head to the tail. He concludes his journal entry on the snake by saying, "My Drawing I Hope Will give you a good Idea of a Rattle Snake although the Heat of the weather Would not permit me to Spend More than 16 hours at it."

Some years later other scientists would corroborate the accuracy of Audubon's famed painting of the rattlesnake attacking the mockingbird nest. They cited numerous instances in which rattlers had been observed entwined around trees; they presented specimens with the very same curved fangs that Audubon had drawn. But the episode was emblematic of the skepticism engendered by Audubon's new approach to portraying birds. He was challenged on any number of counts: was it really true, as he stated, that ruby-throated hummingbirds used their own saliva to attach lichen to their nests? Did a species of yellow water-lily that appeared in one of his paintings even exist? Questioning the details of Audubon paintings became a favorite pastime of his detractors. (Matters weren't helped by Audubon's own lively sense of mischief; he'd once entertained a visiting naturalist with fanciful stories of a species of bird that didn't exist.) But in time Audubon would be vindicated, as one by one the attempts to discredit him would themselves be discredited. Despite his occasional fondness for elaboration and exaggeration, Audubon was extremely serious about his work for *The Birds of America*, once writing, "My work will be a standard one for ages to come." Time, of course, would once again prove him correct.

Left:
Northern Mockingbird

Above:
Savannah Sparrow

Right:
Common Raven

Raven,

CORVUS CORAX,

Male.

Thick Shell-bark Hickory. Juglans laciniosa.

Meadow Lark. STURNUS LUDOVICIANUS. Male 1 Female 2. Gerardia flava.

Drawn from Nature by J.J.Audubon F.R.S.F.L.S.   *Orange-crowned Warbler,* SYLVIA CELATA. *Male,1.Female,2. Vaccinium.*   Engraved, Printed & Coloured by R.Havell.

Left:
Eastern Meadowlark

Above:
Orange-crowned Warbler

N°39.

PLATE. CXCII.

Great cinereous Shrike or Butcher Bird. LANIUS EXCUBITOR.

Above:
Northern Shrike

Right:
Northern Cardinal

PLATE. CLIX

Cardinal Grosbeak.
FRINGILLA CARDINALIS, Bonap.
Male.1. Female.2.
Wild Almond.

Drawn from Nature by J.J.Audubon. F.R.S.F.L.S.

Engraved, Printed & Coloured, by R.Havell, London, 1833.

PLATE VII.

Drawn from Nature by J.J.Audubon, F.R.S. F.L.S.

Engraved by W.H.Lizars Edin.
Retouched by R.Havell Jun. London 1832.

Purple Grakle or Common Crow Blackbird.
QUISCALUS VERSICOLOR, Vieill. Male.1.Female. 2. Maize or Indian Corn, Zea Mays.

Common Grackle

Boat-tailed Grackle.

QUISCALUS MAJOR, Vieill.

Male.1.Female.2.

Live Oak—Quercus virens.

Boat-tailed Grackle

Ferruginous Thrush.
TURDUS RUFUS. Linn.
Male, 1. Female, 2.
Black-jack Oak. Quercus nigra.
Black Snake.

American Goldfinch
FRINGILLA TRISTIS, Linn,
Male, 1. Female, 2.
Common Thistle. Cnicus lanceolatus.

Drawn from Nature and Published by John J.Audubon, F.R.S.F.L.S.

Engraved, Printed & Coloured by R. Havell.

Left:
Brown Thrasher

Above:
American Goldfinch

N°71.

PLATE CCCLIII

Chesnut-backed Titmouse, 1 Male 2 Female.
PARUS RUFESCENS, Townsend.
Drawn from Nature by J. J. Audubon, F.R.S. F.L.S.

Black-capt Titmouse, 3 Male 4 Female.
PARUS ATRICAPILLUS, Wils.
Willow Oak ~ Quercus Phellos, L.

Chesnut-crowned Titmouse, 5 Male 6 Female.
PARUS MINIMUS, Townsend.
(and Nest.)

Engraved, Printed and Coloured by R. Havell 1837.

PLATE CVII.

Canada Jay.
CORVUS CANADENSIS, Linn.
Male 1. Female 2.
White Oak. Quercus alba.

Drawn from Nature by J.J.Audubon F.R.S. F.L.S.

Engraved, Printed, & Coloured by R.Havell. London 1831.

Left:
**Chestnut-backed Chickadee/
Bushtit/ Black-capped
Chickadee**

Above:
Gray Jay

31

Purple Martin.

HIRUNDO PURPUREA. Linn.

Male, 1. Female, 2.

Calabash.

Drawn from Nature and Published by John J. Audubon. F.R.S.F.L.S.

Engraved, Printed, and Coloured by R. Havell.

Above:
Purple Martin

Right:
Snow Bunting

PLATE. CLXXXIX.

Snow Bunting,
EMBERIZA NIVALIS, Linn.
Adult. 1. 2. Young. 3.

Drawn from Nature by J.J.Audubon, F.R.S. F.L.S.

Engraved, Printed & Coloured by R. Havell, 1834.

Sea-side Finch.

FRINGILLA MARITIMA, vis. 1 M & 2 Female, Carolina Rose _Rosa carolina.

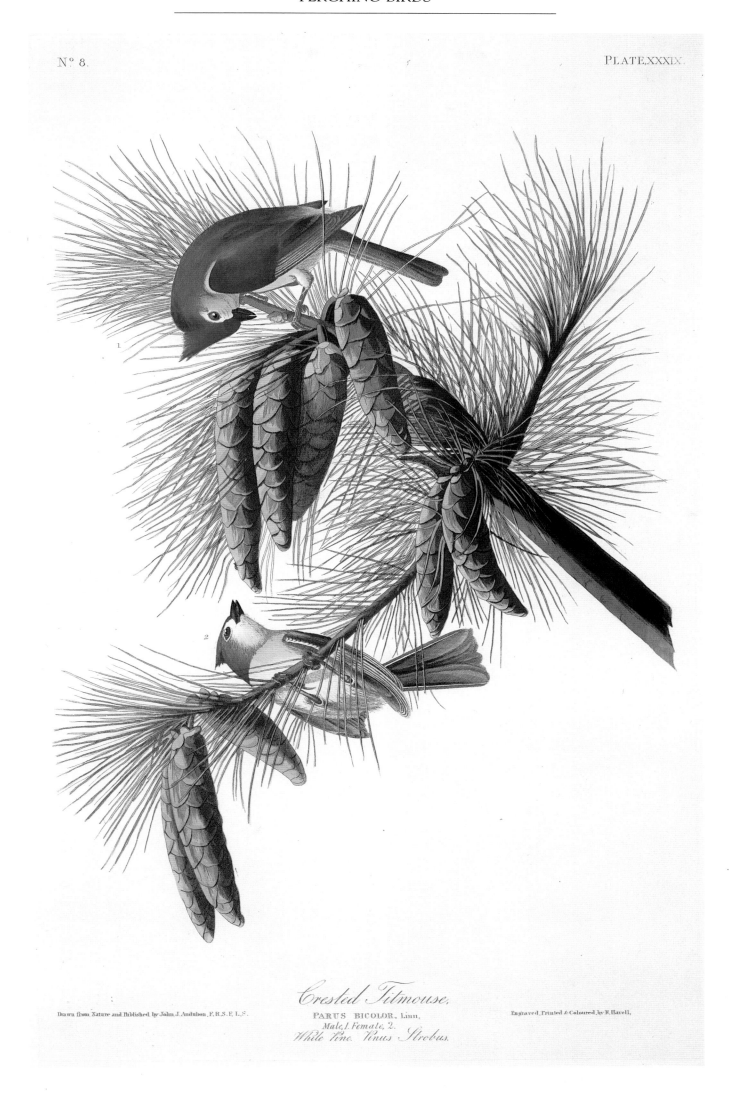

Crested Titmouse.

Drawn from Nature and Published by John J. Audubon, F.R.S.E.L.S.   PARUS BICOLOR, Linn,   Engraved, Printed & Coloured, by R. Havell,
Male, 1. Female, 2.
White Pine. Pinus Strobus.

Left:
Seaside Sparrow

Above:
Tufted Titmouse

Rose-breasted Grosbeak, FRINGILLA LUDOVICIANA. Bonap. *Male, 1. Female, 2. Young in autum, 3. Young, 4. Ground Hemlock, Taxus canadensis.*

Rose-breasted Grosbeak

Baltimore Oriole. ICTERUS BALTIMORE. Daud. Adult Male, 1. Male two years old, 2. Female, 3. Tulip Tree Liriodendron tulipifera

Northern Oriole

37

Golden Eagle. FALCO CHRYSAETOS. Female adult. Northern Hare.

BIRDS OF PREY

More than one person who encountered Audubon took special note of his "eagle eyes," and it wasn't an idle metaphor: just a glimpse of a striking bird was enough to send him off in pursuit, his shotgun in hand. When it came to birds, Audubon was the predator, and they were the prey.

While hunting was certainly an acceptable part of life in the young country, there were times when Audubon's cold-bloodedness would prove unsettling to those around him. A neighbor in Louisiana wrote of the methodical way Audubon once stalked a bald eagle. Early in the day Audubon had climbed a magnolia tree to examine the eagle's nest, and he knew that sooner or later the bird would return to investigate. Audubon waited for him: ". . . there the poor bird sat, until Audubon coolly loaded his rifle with a bullet, and then like a serpent, on his belly, he had time to noiselessly, and un-observed even by the keen eye of the bird of Jove, crawl within gunshot . . . I could see the bird, standing erect, and with earnest gaze looking toward his nest, his mate and his young in the distant swamp." A shot rang out, the man said, and the bird fell dead. "I admired Audubon's spirit, knowledge and pluck, but I must confess I felt sorry for the poor bird."

Audubon didn't kill without a purpose, however. Within hours he had stuffed the eagle and arranged it in such a way that it seemed to have regained its life. He even placed a magnolia branch behind the bird to lend the scene still more authenticity.

While *The Birds of America* introduced more than three dozen species that had been previously undocumented, Audubon occasionally became so caught up in his urgent quest to discover new birds that he acted too hastily. An episode involving another bald eagle is perhaps the most famous instance of this rush to record new species. During one of his early trips in the southern United States, Audubon came upon what he thought was a new species of eagle, one with feathers that were entirely brown and black. In a burst of patriotism he christened it the Washington sea eagle or the Bird of Washington. *The Birds of America* contains one plate of a "White-headed Sea Eagle, or Bald Eagle," and another of the "Washington Sea Eagle." In fact, they were one and the same bird, *Haliaeetus leucocephalus*. Audubon had mistaken an immature female bald eagle for a new species.

Though his formal education in science was negligible – Audubon had been schooled largely in the gentlemanly arts – he was no stranger to scientific method. One of his most noted experiments, and most controversial, involved birds of prey. It was generally accepted in Audubon's time that it was a keen sense of smell that enabled vultures to home in on rotting carcasses. Audubon was not convinced. More than once in his excursions through the wilds he had noted that a stealthy approach would enable him to come remarkably close to a vulture. But as soon as the bird would sight him, off it would fly, startled. The conclusion was obvious: vultures relied less on their sense of smell than their vision.

Audubon devised a plan to test his theory. He cleaned a deerskin of all traces of flesh, stuffed it with hay so that it once again looked like a deer, and then placed it in a field and waited. Within minutes a vulture appeared and settled in for a feeding session. It poked around first one end of the "deer," then the other, in search of meat. Finally, finding none, the bird flew off.

Audubon tried another experiment to confirm his findings. This time he concealed the carcass of a pig inside a log. Even as dogs, which had quickly sniffed out the odor of decay, began consuming the rotting flesh, vultures flew overhead, oblivious. That was all the proof Audubon needed: it was clear that for a vulture the success of a hunt depended far less on smell than on sight. But old ideas die hard, and when Audubon presented his theory before a learned society in London in the mid-1820s, he was roundly criticized. Several years later his good friend John Bachman conducted some additional experiments designed to squelch Audubon's critics. He reported that vultures even attacked a painting of a sheep, and eventually the uproar died down. He may not have considered himself a scientist, but through observation and experiment Audubon had succeeded in refuting one of the most commonly accepted maxims about birds of his time.

Left:
Golden Eagle

40

Great Horned Owl

STRIX VIRGINIANA, Gmel.

Male & Female.

Drawn from Nature & Published by John J. Aud. Jun. F.R.S.C.L.S.   Engraved, Printed & Coloured by J. Havell.

Turkey Buzzard.

CATHARTES AURA,

Male 1.Young. 2.

Left:
Great Horned Owl

Above:
Turkey Vulture

No. 7.

White-headed Eagle. FALCO LEUCOCEPHALUS, Linn.

PLATE XXXI.

Cat-fish.

Engraved, Printed & Coloured, by R. Havell.

Bald Eagle

Marsh Hawk.
FALCO CYANEUS.

Iceland or Jer Falcon.
FALCO ISLANDICUS. *Lath.*

Left:
Northern Harrier

Above:
Gyrfalcon

45

Peregrine Falcon

PLATE XVI.

Hawk, FALCO PEREGRINUS. Gmel. *Male,* 1 *Female,* 2. *Green-winged Teal and Gadwal.*

Engraved, Printed & Coloured by R. Havell

Black Warrior.
FALCO HARLANI.
Male 1. Female 2.

Red-tailed Hawk. FALCO BOREALIS, Gmel. *Male 1. Female 2. American Hare Lepus americanus.*

Left:
Red-tailed Hawk

Above:
Red-tailed Hawk

No. 29

PLATE CXLII

American Sparrow Hawk. FALCO SPARVERIUS Linn. *Male, 1 Female 2. Butter-nut or Walte walnut Juglans cinerea*

Drawn from Nature by J.J.Audubon, F.R.S. F.L.S.

Engraved,Printed & Coloured by R. Havell London.

Above:
American Kestrel

Right:
Great Gray Owl

Great Cinereous Owl.
STRIX CINEREOUS, Gmelin
Female Adult.

Common Buzzard?
BUTEO VULGARIS.
Female
Marsh Hawk. Female
Lepus Zaleatus. Bachman

Drawn from Nature by J.J.Audubon F. R. S. F. L. S.

Engraved, Printed and Coloured by R.Havell 1837

Above:
Swainson's Hawk

Right:
Rough-legged Hawk

Rough-legged Falcon.

FALCO LAGOPUS.

Male.

American Swallow-tailed Kite

PLATE LXXII.

l Hawk,

'S , Linn,

Engraved Printed & Coloured by R.Havell.

Goshawk.
FALCO PALUMBARIUS. Linn.
Adult Male 1. Young. 2.

Stanley Hawk.
FALCO STANLEII. Aud.
Adult. 3.

Fish Hawk or Osprey, FALCO HALIÆTUS, *Mate. Weak Fish.*

Left:
Northern Goshawk/Cooper's Hawk

Above:
Osprey

Red-shouldered Hawk.
FALCO LINEATUS, Gmel.
Male 1. Female 2.

Above:
Red-Shouldered Hawk

Right:
Snowy Owl

Snowy Owl, STRIX NYCTEA - Linn. Male 1. Female 2.

Snowy Egret

WATER BIRDS

The sight that greeted Audubon on the first leg of his long-awaited trip to Labrador in 1833 was one of the most remarkable of a life spent observing nature. As his schooner approached Nova Scotia the crew hastened to point out a huge rock which appeared to be covered in snow. But appearances can be deceiving, as the veteran sailors knew. Audubon wrote of the experience this way in his journal: " . . . the snow . . . seemed two or three feet thick . . . I rubbed my eyes, and took my spy-glass, and instantly the strange picture stood before me. They were indeed birds, and such a mass of birds, and of such a size as I never saw before." Coming from so seasoned an observer of birds as Audubon, the description is that much more powerful. What appeared for all the world to be a snow-covered rock was in fact a mass of white gannets, just one of the many new birds Audubon came upon on this trip to the far north.

The journey to the harsh climate of Labrador was not easy on Audubon, but it gave him the opportunity to study a number of water birds which had eluded him thus far. Moreover, it allowed him to complete paintings of other species that he had already sketched during their migratory stopovers in Louisiana during the winters. Audubon could observe the birds' plumage in the cold conditions of Labrador, examine their habitats, and note the ways in which they adjusted to what Audubon clearly considered an inhospitable region. In a typical journal entry during the trip, he writes, "The weather shocking, rainy, foggy, dark and cold."

Louisiana, with its swamps and bayous filled with wildlife, had provided Audubon with a number of species for *The Birds of America*, and his brief trip to a New Jersey swamp after his return from England in 1829 had also been profitable from an artistic and scientific standpoint. But by the early 1830s Audubon was becoming obsessed with the need for his book to contain paintings of every known species of American bird. "The fact is I am growing old too fast, alas!" (Audubon was actually not even 50). "I feel it, and yet work I will, and may God grant me life to see the last plate of my mammoth work finished."

The trip to Labrador enabled Audubon to expand the scope of his book significantly. Water birds, especially, were abundant there – fine specimens of guillemots, puffins, razor-billed auks, ducks, and gulls. The pleasures of observing them all helped Audubon forget just how unpleasant aspects of the journey had been. "The little ring-plover rearing its delicate and tender young; the eider duck swimming man-of-war-like amid her floating brood, like the guard-ship of a most valuable convoy; . . . the crowds of sea-birds in search of places wherein to repose or to feed. I say how beautiful all this . . . "

Audubon and his assistants would head out in the mornings with their guns, determined to bring back as many birds as they could bag; his work had always relied on freshly shot specimens. Over 200 birds were killed during the course of the trip, and Audubon succeeded in finishing 23 new paintings. But even with years of experience behind him, the task of reproducing nature still didn't come easy. The loon, he noted in his journal after spending an entire day attempting to draw one, is "a most difficult bird to imitate."

Despite his own occasional tendency to overkill, the Labrador trip reinforced Audubon's concern for the fate of many of the birds he had encountered throughout the years. The island was home to men called "eggers," who made their living by stealing eggs from nests and then selling them. Audubon, who could hardly proclaim himself innocent of taking life from birds, objected less to the eggers' occupation than to the careless way they went about their work. For these "destructive pirates," as Audubon called them, it wasn't enough merely to steal the eggs; more often than not they destroyed the birds as well for no reason other than brutality. These journal entries demonstrate why Audubon's name is now associated with wildlife conservation. "This war of extermination cannot last many years more. The eggers themselves will be the first to repent the entire disappearance of myriads of birds that made the coast of Labrador their summer residence." Later, Audubon asks plaintively, "Where can I go now and find nature undisturbed?"

Overleaf:
Mallard

Mallard Duck.

PLATE. CCXXI

Engraved, Printed, & Coloured by R.Havell. 1834.

AAS . 1 Males. 2 Females

Belted Kingfisher, ALCEDO ALCYON. Linn. Male.1,2.Female.3.

Belted Kingfisher

Bonaparte's Gull

Nº 59

Drawn from Nature by J.J.Audubon F.R.S.F.L.S.

Horned Puffin

PLATE CCXCIII

Large billed Puffin.
MORMON GLACIALIS, Leach.
1. Male. 2. Female.

Engraved, Printed, & Coloured, by R.Havell, 1836

Overleaf:
Trumpeter Swan

N° 82.

Drawn from Nature by J.J.Audubon, F.R.S. F.L.S.

Trumpeter
CYGNUS BUCCINAT
Adult.

PLATE CCCCVI

Engraved, Printed & Coloured by R.Havell,1837.

Nº 64

PLATE CCCXVI

Black-bellied Darter
PLOTUS ANHINGA, L.

Canada Goose
ANSER CANADENSIS, *Vieill*
Male, 1. Female, 2.

Left:
Anhinga

Above:
Canada Goose

Nº 62

Drawn from Nature by J. J. Audubon, F. R. S.   F. L. S.

Common Loon

PLATE CCCVI.

Engraved, Printed & Coloured by R.Havell 1836.

Great Northern Diver or Loon.
COLYMBUS GLACIALIS, L.
Adult 1. Young in Winter 2.

Whooping Crane.
CRUS AMERICANA.
Young.

Black-Backed Gull.
LARUS MARINUS.

Left:
Sandhill Crane

Above:
Great Black-backed Gull

N.º 44.

PLATE CCXIX.

Engraved. Printed,& Coloured. by R. Havell. 1834.

Overleaf:
Northern Gannet

Drawn from Nature by J. J. Audubon, F.R.S. F.L.S.

Black Backed Gull.
LARUS MARINUS.

Left:
Sandhill Crane

Above:
Great Black-backed Gull

N.º 44.

Drawn from Nature by J.J.Audubon, F.R.S. F.L.S.

Black Guillemot,
URIA GRYLLE, Lath.
1.Adult summer plumage. 2. D.º Winter plumage. 3. Young.

Black Guillemot

PLATE CCXIX.

Engraved, Printed, & Coloured, by R. Havell. 1834.

Overleaf:
Northern Gannet

Drawn from Nature by J.J Audubon, F.R.S. F.L.S.

Engraved, Printed and Coloured by R. Havell, 1836.

Brown Pelican.
PELECANUS FUSCUS.
Male Adult.

N°. 50.

PLATE. CCL.

Drawn from Nature by J.J. Audubon, F.R.S. F.L.S.

Engraved, Printed, & Coloured, by R. Havell, London. 1835.

Arctic Tern.
STERNA ARCTICA.

Left: **Brown Pelican**

Above:
Arctic Tern

Overleaf:
King Eider

Nº 56.

Drawn from Nature by J.J. Audubon, F.R.S. F.L.S.

PLATE CCLXXVI

King Duck.

LA SPECTABILIS,

Male 1. Female 2.

Engraved Printed & Coloured. by R. Havell. 1835.

N.º 60

84

Drawn from Nature by J.J.Audubon, F.R.S. F.L.S.

Barnacle Goose

PLATE CCXCVI

85

Barnacle Goose.
ANSER LEUCOPSIS,
1 Male, 2 Female.

Engraved Printed & Coloured by R. Havell 1836.

Herring Gull.
LARUS ARGENTATUS.

Above:
Herring Gull

Right:
Whooping Crane

Whooping Crane. GRUS AMERICANA. Adult Male.

Long-billed Curlew

PLATE CCXXXI

W. NUMENIUS LONGIROSTRIS. 1 Male 2 Female. City of Charleston.

Engraved, Printed, & Coloured, by R. Havell 1834.

Overleaf:
White-tailed Tropicbird

Nº 53.

Drawn from Nature by J.J. Audubon F.R.S. F.L.S.

Tro
PHAETO

PLATE CCLXII.

2

Engraved, Printed,& Coloured, by R. Havell. 1835.

rd.

EUS, Linn

Wild Turkey. MELEAGRIS GALLOPAVO, Linn., Male. American Cane.

PLATE C CLXII.

rd.

E U S . Linn

Engraved, Printed,& Coloured. by R. Havell. 1835.

PLATE

Wild Turkey, MELEAGRIS GALLOPAVO, Linn, Male. American Cane. Virgin macrosperma.

Engraved by W. H. Lizars
Retouched by R. Havell, Jun.

A MISCELLANY

The most famous of all of Audubon's bird paintings was the one he selected to serve as the frontispiece of *The Birds of America*: the Wild Turkey (Audubon's title was Great American Cock). The painting is remarkable not just for its beauty – the delicately shaded burnt oranges and umbers of the bird's feathers are made even more striking by the soothing greens of the bamboo in the background – but for its symbolism. By the early 1800s the wild turkey had come to represent the vigor and strength of the new nation. The bird was a wildly flamboyant species and Audubon had cannily posed it to show off its independent nature. The turkey is strutting forward confidently, but its head is turned imperiously toward the back so it can keep a keen eye on everything around it. It was an apt metaphor for the United States.

The wild turkey was the first of Audubon's paintings to be transformed into a finished print by William Lizars, the Scottish engraver, and though the partnership with Lizars would prove ill-fated when his firm's colorists went on strike, this initial effort was a success. Upon his first inspection of the wild turkey, which Lizars completed on November 28, 1826, Audubon noted, "Saw to-day the first proof of the first engraving of my American Birds, and was very well pleased with its appearance." The wild turkey plate was an auspicious debut for the volume Audubon proposed. Several years later he would open the *Ornithological Biography*, his text for *The Birds of America*, with a "life history" of the same bird.

Like so many of the birds Audubon painted, the wild turkey had been discovered by Audubon in the Louisiana woods during the happy times he spent in that region with Lucy before heading off to England in search of subscribers to his great book. The bayou country of the American South was to provide Audubon with some of his best hunting, and best working conditions as well. After bagging the day's birds Audubon would hasten back to his quarters to draw. Early on he had discovered that the colors of the birds' plumage faded fast, and so it was imperative for him to work quickly.

His sure sense of color had been heightened by the close inspection he gave to beautifully muted and shaded bits of old wood and moss and other objects he had collected from nature over the course of a lifetime. His lovely painting of a pair of passenger pigeons shows how he used the colors of the birds' natural surroundings to enhance the scene. The rosy hues of the male's chest are echoed in the bark of the tree in which the birds are perched.

Audubon had always intended *The Birds of America* to be a comprehensive work, and he tried to include not just a single bird of each species but representatives of each stage of the species' development: male, female, young, mature. Most often he included several birds in each painting. The wild turkey stands alone, however, its majesty emphasized by the solitary pose. Audubon would depict other members of the species in a later plate. In this painting the female turkey marches headlong through a field, her brood of young chicks tumbling along underfoot as she goes.

Audubon had painted the wild turkey in 1825, after a number of unsuccessful attempts to do the bird justice, and it represents the artist at the height of his powers. Even those who complained that many of Audubon's paintings were overwrought, filled with not just drama but melodrama, would be hard pressed to fault the striking dignity of his wild turkey. The range of Audubon's bird paintings was remarkable – they included every bird from the tiny ruby-throated hummingbird to the elegant trumpeter swan – but it was his wild turkey that would set the masterly tone for what was to come in *The Birds of America*.

Left:
Wild Turkey

Ivory-billed Woodpecker. PICUS PRINCIPALIS. Linn. Male.1.Female.2.3.

Left:
Ivory-billed Woodpecker

Above:
Mourning Dove

Nº 34.

Drawn from Nature by J.J.Audubon. F.R.S. F.L.S

Key West Quail-Dove

PLATE. CLXVII.

Key west Pigeon.
COLUMBA MONTANA.
Male 1. Female 2

Engraved, Printed & Coloured by R. Havell, London 18

Overleaf:
Wild Turkey (female w/chicks)

Wild Turkey. MELEAGR

N.D. Linu *Female and Young.*

Engraved by W.H.Lizars.
Retouched by R.Havell Junr.

Passenger Pigeon,
COLUMBA MIGRATORIA, Linn.
Male, 1, Female, 2.

Passenger Pigeon

Ruby-throated Humming Bird.

TROCHILUS COLUBRIS. Linn.

Male, 1. Female, 2. Young, 3.

Trumpet flower. Bignonia Radicans.

Drawn from Nature and Published by John J. Audubon, F.R.S. F.L.S.

Engraved, Printed, & Coloured, by R. Havell.

Ruby-throated Hummingbird

Maria's Woodpecker.
PICUS MARTINI, Aud.
1 Male. 2 Female.

Three-toed Woodpecker.
PICUS HIRSUTUS, Vieil.
3 Male. 4 Female.

Phillips' Woodpecker.
PICUS PHILLIPSI, Aud.
5 and 6 Males.

Canadian Woodpecker.
PICUS CANADENSIS, Buff.
7 Male.

Harris's Woodpecker.
PICUS HARRISI, Aud.
8 Male. 9 Female.

Audubon's Woodpecker.
PICUS AUDUBONI, Trudeau.
10 Male.

Nº 11.

PLATE LII.

Chuck-wills Widow,

CAPRIMULGUS CAROLINENSIS, Briss.

Male 1. Female 2.

Harlequin Snake.

Drawn from Nature, and Published by John J. Audubon, F.R.S.F.L.S.

Engraved, Printed, & Coloured by R. Havell.

Left:
Hairy Woodpecker/Three-toed Woodpecker

Above:
Chuck-will's-widow

N.º 8.

PLATE XXXVII.

Golden-winged Woodpecker
PICUS AURATUS, Linn.
Males. 1. Females. 2.

Drawn from Nature and Published by John J. Audubon, F.R.S.E.L.S.

Engraved, Printed & Coloured, by R. Havell.

Above:
Northern Flicker

Right:
Bohemian Waxwing

Nº 73.

PLATE CCCLXIII.

Bohemian Chatterer.

BOMBYCILLA GARRULA.

Male 1. Female 2.

Pyrus Americana Canadian Service Tree.

Drawn from Nature by J.J. Audubon, F.R.S. F.L.S.

Engraved, Printed and Coloured by R. Havell. 1837

Overleaf: **Rock Ptarmigan**

N.º 74.

Drawn from Nature by J. J. Audubon, F.R.S. F.L.S.

Roc
TETRAO I
Male in Winter. 1 . Fe

PLATE CCCLXVIII.

Engraved, Printed and Coloured by R Havell. 1837.

ous.

S, Leach.

ge 2. Young in August; 3.

PLATE XXVI.

Carolina Parrot.

PSITTACUS CAROLINENSIS, Linn.
Males 1, females 2, young 3.
Cockle-bur Xanthium Strumarium.

Drawn from Nature & Published by John J. Audubon, F.R.S.E.L.S.

Engraved Printed & Coloured by R. Havell.

Left:
Carolina Parakeet

Above:
Black-billed Cuckoo

N° 9.

Drawn from Nature & Published by John J. Audubon F.R.S.F.L.S.

Ruffed Grouse

Ruffed Grouse. TETRAO UMBELLUS, Linn. Male 1. 2 Female. 3.

LIST OF COLOR PLATES

Acknowledgments
The author and publisher would like to thank the following people who helped in the preparation of this book: Don Longabucco, the designer; Susan Bernstein, the editor; and Rita Longabucco, the picture editor.

Picture Credits
All color prints by John James Audubon courtesy of the Library of Congress, Rare Book Collection.
Museum of the City of New York, The J. Clarence Davies Collection: 16.
Courtesy of The New-York Historical Society, New York City: 8(top left), 9(left), 12, 13(right), 17.
Courtesy of the Princeton University Library: 8(bottom right), 13(left), 14(bottom right).
UPI/Bettmann Newsphotos: 6, 9(right).